THE GIN GAME

THE GIN GAME

D. L. COBURN

DRAMA BOOK SPECIALISTS (PUBLISHERS)
NEW YORK

Library of Congress Cataloging in Publication Data

Coburn, D.L.
      The gin game.

      I. Title.   812'.5'4   78-16784
PS3553.O233G5
ISBN 0-89676-002-2

Manufactured in the United States of America

To my son, Donn Christopher,
whose urging led me to return to and complete this play.
And to my sweet daughter Kimberly.

THE GIN GAME *was first presented on Broadway on October 6, 1977, by The Schubert Organization, produced by Hume Cronyn and Mike Nichols, at the John Golden Theatre, New York City, with the following cast:*

FONSIA DORSEY   Jessica Tandy
WELLER MARTIN   Hume Cronyn

Directed by Mike Nichols

Setting by David Mitchell
Costumes by Bill Walker
Lighting by Ronald Wallace

*Production Supervisor/*Nina Seely

Originally presented by The Long Wharf Theatre, New Haven, co-produced by Icarus Productions, Inc., and The Cronyn Company.

THE GIN GAME *was awarded the Pulitzer Prize for the Best Play in 1978.*

THE GIN GAME *was given its first performance in Los Angeles, California, on September 24, 1976, by American Theatre Arts, with the following cast:*

FONSIA DORSEY   Carol Lawson Locatell
WELLER MARTIN   John Terry Bell

Artistic Director/Don Eitner
Director/Kip Niven

CAST OF CHARACTERS

FONSIA DORSEY, an elderly woman, 65-70 years old
WELLER MARTIN, an elderly man, 70-75 years old

*The action takes place in a home for the aged in the early
1970s. The setting is the sunporch of the Bentley Nursing and
Convalescent Home, and is the same throughout the play.*

ACT ONE
Scene 1: Sunday afternoon, Visitors' Day. Springtime.
Scene 2: Sunday afternoon, one week later.

ACT TWO
Scene 1: The following evening, shortly after dinner.
Scene 2: The following Sunday afternoon.

THE GIN GAME

As Leaden As The Aftermath Of Wine

As leaden as the aftermath of wine
Is the dead mirth of my delirious days;
And as wine waxes strong with age, so weighs
More heavily the past on my decline.
My path is dim. The future's troubled sea
Foretokens only toil and grief to me.
But oh! my friends, I do not ask to die!
I crave more life, more dreams, more agony!
Midmost the care, the panic, the distress,
I know that I shall taste of happiness.
Once more I shall be drunk on strains divine,
Be moved to tears by musings that are mine;
And haply when the last sad hour draws nigh,
Love with a farewell smile may gild the sky.

—Alexander Sergheievich Pushkin

Reprinted from *Lost Lectures* by Maurice Baring,
Alfred A. Knopf, Inc., New York, 1932.

ACT ONE

SCENE 1

(The scene is the sunporch of a home for the aged. Shafts of sunlight punctuate a room laden with plants. French doors provide access to the porch from rear center stage. To either side of the french doors is a series of windows from the main living room of the home. Large screened windows frame the stage at the extreme left and right. To the left, a porch swing or a glider is surrounded by potted palms and other large plants. To the rear stage left, behind the porch swing, stands a tall, stately bookcase, cluttered with seldom read books. There is the musty feeling of dust swirling through sunbeams, and it is obviously early afternoon of a brilliantly sunny day. The season is spring . . . the day, Sunday, visitors' day at the home. From the main living room we hear the excited greetings and chatter of the residents and their relatives and friends. In the middle of the room there is a card table and two facing chairs. As the curtain rises, WELLER *is seated at the card table, playing solitaire.*

FONSIA *enters through the french doors, seemingly lost in thought. She starts for a moment at unexpectedly seeing* WELLER.*)*

FONSIA *(Embarrassed)* Oh, I . . . I didn't think anyone was out here.

WELLER   I'm sorry I startled you.

FONSIA   Oh, it wasn't you . . . it was just—my mind was a thousand miles away.
(She turns and moves stage left, wandering from flower

pot to flower pot, pausing now and then for a closer inspection. Upon reaching the screened window stage left, she tires of the plants and stares wistfully into space. WELLER *studies* FONSIA *midway through her walk, then continues his game of solitaire. She, however, is now his focal point of interest.)*

WELLER   You're rather new here, aren't you?

FONSIA *(She turns to him)*   Three weeks.

WELLER   It takes some adjustment.

FONSIA *(Suddenly interested)*   How long have you been here?

WELLER   Couple of months.

FONSIA   Well, you're kinda new here too.

WELLER   In a way. Of course it's not the first time I've lived in. They're all pretty much alike.

FONSIA   I came here to Bentley because they're supposed to have constant care.

WELLER   What's wrong with you—if . . . if you don't mind my asking.

FONSIA   Oh, my . . . Lord no, I don't mind. I've got chronic diabetes.

WELLER   Diabetes mellitus.

FONSIA   Is there something wrong with you? . . . I mean are you sick?

WELLER   Oh my, I should say *so*. I have one of the most

advanced cases of *old age* in the history of medical science. *(Pause.)* The mortality rate's incredible.

FONSIA I just thought there might have been something you were getting treatment for.

WELLER No. You don't need anything special to qualify for Bentley. Old age is sufficient.

FONSIA Have you ever lived at the Presbyterian Home?

WELLER No.

FONSIA *(Wistfully)* That's the place I really wanted to go to.

WELLER Why didn't you?

FONSIA Well, they have a rather unusual financial setup.

WELLER What's that?

FONSIA You have to give them all your money.

WELLER That's the place! That's the goddamn place. *(He slaps the cards he holds to the table for emphasis.)* That's the place where you have to give them all your money. *(He gets to his feet and paces the small area around the card table during the subsequent comments. He has a slight limp, but uses the cane he constantly has in hand, more as a prop than an actual aid to walking.)* The Presbyterian Home . . . Christ, what a racket. Think of all the poor bastards out there right now. Thinking they're working for themselves, when really they're working for the Presbyterian Home.

FONSIA *(Defensively)*   They don't *have* to go there.

WELLER   Oh. Hell no. They don't have to go there. They don't have to go anywhere if they don't want to. *(He reflects on this for a moment.)* That's a damn lie. You do have to go somewhere. If you live long enough, sooner or later you end up in one of these places.

FONSIA   I guess you're right. 'Course, if you were rich enough . . .

WELLER   Don't be deluded by money either. I've seen some very wealthy people in old age homes. Loneliness—simple as that.

FONSIA   That's why I wanted to go to the Presbyterian Home. See, I have friends over there I've known all my life.

WELLER *(Challenging)*   Why didn't you give them your money?

FONSIA   I just couldn't bring myself to do that.

WELLER   Who the hell *could*? It's unreasonable to expect a person to turn over everything they have—I don't care how nice the place is. You're entitled to some personal property. Even the welfare department lets you keep twenty-five hundred dollars.

FONSIA   You might be right—I'm sure they have their side of it too. It's just a matter of opinion, I guess.

WELLER   It's not a matter of opinion. *(He walks back to the card table, seats himself, and pretends to resume his*

game of solitaire.) A fact . . . is a fact. *(Very long pause.*
WELLER, *nicer now.)* Do you play cards?

FONSIA   Oh, it's been years since I've played any cards.
I used to love to play. I could sit and play rummy or
pinochle 'til two o'clock in the morning. *(Bemused.)* If
my mother'd ever known I was doing that, she'd a
killed me. We were raised old-time Methodist, you
know. And we considered card playin' a sin.

WELLER   The only sin in card playing is drawing to an
inside straight. And even that's not a sin if you fill it.
(He laughs at his own twist of logic.)

FONSIA   That's poker you're talking about, isn't it?

WELLER   What? Oh, the inside straight—yes, that's
poker.

FONSIA   I never did see much sense to that. For one
thing, I could never keep straight what beats what.

WELLER   Did you ever play gin?
(WELLER shuffles the cards.)

FONSIA   Is gin and rummy the same? Seems to me they
called it gin rummy.

WELLER   It's the same principle. I keep score on what's
known as the Hollywood basis. Here, sit down. I'll
show you. *(FONSIA walks to the card table. As she is about
to take a seat,* WELLER *stands.)* By the way, I'm Weller
Martin.

FONSIA   I'm Fonsia Dorsey.

WELLER   Well, pleased to meet you, Fonsia. *(They sit.)*

Now then . . . the first thing we do . . . I think you'll enjoy this . . . is deal the cards . . . ten for me . . . and eleven for you. *(Dealing ritual.)* One, one. Two, two. Three, three. Four, four. Five, five. Six, six. Seven, seven. Eight, eight. Nine, nine, Ten, ten. And eleven for you. Now the reason I'm giving you eleven is because you have to discard one to start the game.

FONSIA   All the same kind go together . . . like kings or eights.

WELLER   That's right—and a sequence *in the same* suit . . . like eight, nine, ten of diamonds, or ace, king, queen of hearts. But it has to be at least three in a row.

FONSIA   Do I lay them down as soon as I get them?

WELLER   No . . . uh-uh. Hold on until everything you have in your hand goes together, except one card. Then you discard that card . . . and say GIN.

FONSIA   Oh. Well, that's a little different. We used to play that you laid them down as you got them. You know, three of a kind or whatever.

WELLER   Well, this is the accepted way. You go anywhere in the world and this is the way that gin will be played.

FONSIA   I accept it.

WELLER   Good.

FONSIA   I mean I like the idea. You sort of surprise the other person when you get gin.

WELLER That's right. Oh . . . and there's one other way of going out. That's by knocking.

FONSIA Knocking?

WELLER Yes. All that means is that if all the cards you have that don't match add up to less than ten points, you can knock.

FONSIA *(She doesn't understand)* Uh-huh.

WELLER *(To himself)* Did I say that right? *(He takes the cards from her hand.)* Here, let me show you. Say, for example . . . Well, all your cards are matched up except this six and this two. If you want to you can knock. You'd say, "I knock with eight points." Now if I have more than eight points, you win. If I have less than eight . . . I win. Do you understand that?

FONSIA I think so . . . but I think I'll just stick to the gin part of the game at first.

WELLER That's all right. You think you've got it now?

FONSIA Yes, I think so.

WELLER All right, good, then let's play. *(He marks out a score sheet.)* Fonsia . . . Weller . . . Fonsia . . . Weller . . . Fonsia . . . Weller. *(FONSIA is confused by this. WELLER looks up, noticing her confusion.)* Oh, don't worry. I'll keep score all the time. Some people play to 150 points, but we'll just play to 100 points. Still bona fide, only faster. Here, give me those to shuffle up and we'll start all over again.
(WELLER picks up the cards and shuffles them.)

FONSIA   This is exciting! I'm actually enjoying myself. If you'd told me fifteen minutes ago, that . . .

WELLER *(Dealing)*   One, one. Two, two. Three, three. Four, four. Five, five. Six, six. Seven, seven. Eight, eight. Nine, nine. Ten, ten. And eleven for you.

FONSIA   . . . that fifteen minutes ago, I'd be playing *gin rummy* with someone . . .
(They pick up their cards, arrange them in their hands, and begin the play of the game. Throughout the following dialogue, the play of the hand proceeds normally.)

WELLER   I can see your cards.

FONSIA *(Continuing)*   I thought this was going to be an awful day.

WELLER   Visitors' day?

FONSIA   Um-hum.

WELLER   Do you have any family?

FONSIA   Oh, my yes. Of course. I have a son almost forty-five years old . . . Larry.

WELLER   Mr. Dorsey passed on?

FONSIA   We were only married four years. We were divorced when Larry was two.

WELLER   Oh, I see.

FONSIA   Actually Walter did pass on not too long ago. Then I have a sister, Hattie . . . she lives in Ottawa. I haven't seen her in fifteen years.

WELLER   Does your son live here in town?

FONSIA   No. Ah . . . he and his wife make their home in Denver.

WELLER   Denver! Well, I guess you don't get to see much of him either.

FONSIA   No. It's been over a year since he's been home. Then I have two lovely grandchildren, both boys. Steven's twelve . . . and Larry Junior . . . Oh, my Lord, Larry must be sixteen. Almost a man.

WELLER   They grow up quickly.

FONSIA   Do you have any children?

WELLER   Yes, I . . .

FONSIA   Wait a minute. I'm sorry, Weller, I think I'm sitting here with gin in my hand already. Let's see, there's four of the kings, three nines, and the five, six, seven of spades. I've got the eight, too. I guess I just discard that.

WELLER   *(Patronizing)* That's right. Very good. Very good. Now, you get twenty-five for gin, and I'm stuck with the eight and nine of hearts, so that's seventeen more. So you're forty-two points to the good. (WELLER *notes score pad.*) Fonsia, forty-two points in the first game.

FONSIA   Oh, I'm sorry. I get to talking and I forget what I'm doing.

WELLER   *(He gathers the cards and begins to shuffle them.)* You played that hand very well.

FONSIA   Beginner's luck, I guess.

WELLER   No, really. A lot of people would've discarded those two kings right away . . . but you held on to them and filled them out.

FONSIA   I didn't realize there was that much strategy to it.

WELLER   There most certainly is. Anyone who says gin is nothing but luck doesn't know what the game is all about.

FONSIA   Oh, I was just about to ask you.

WELLER   *(Dealing)*   One, one. Two, two. Three, three. Four, four. Five, five. Six, six. Seven, seven. Eight, eight. Nine, nine. Ten, ten. Eleven for you.

FONSIA   *(Continues)*   To ask you about your children.
(The play of the cards proceeds. The dialogue may be spaced to allow a reasonable time to transpire before FONSIA *announces gin. A normal gin hand takes two to five minutes.)*

WELLER   I have three children . . . all grown, of course. Two sons and a daughter.

FONSIA   Do you hear from them much?

WELLER   No. Actually, we've lost touch over the years.

FONSIA   That's awful . . . I mean, to lose touch that way.

WELLER   That happened many years ago. I'm also divorced, and their mother didn't exactly encourage a close relationship between us. She moved—she and the children—to another city. I had a business established so I couldn't follow them. Eventually she re-married, so that was more or less the end of that.

FONSIA How dreadful.

WELLER Well, in those days the courts gave the woman a great deal of power in a divorce settlement—there was very little I could do about it.

FONSIA I'm sorry that happened to you. Of course, that's exactly what some men deserve. Seems like there's no justice. Now that would've suited the one I had just right.

WELLER It doesn't suit anyone just right.

FONSIA Oh, I don't mean you, Weller. Lord no. I'm talking about the man I married.

WELLER I know that . . . and I'm saying I wouldn't wish it on him either.

FONSIA Well, if you knew the hell I went through, you'd change your tune mighty fast on that. *(Pause.)* Gin!

WELLER So it is. So it is. I'm stuck with twenty-three. No more lessons for you. (WELLER *marks score.*)

FONSIA That was lucky—I got everything I needed right away.

WELLER You certainly did.

FONSIA It's pleasant out here in a way. The rooms are so small, though. Trying to get all your worldly possessions in a little ten-foot-square box . . . makes you realize . . .

WELLER   Realize what? *(He deals.)* One, one. Two, two.
Three, three. Four, four. Five, five. Six, six. Seven,
seven. Eight, eight. Nine, nine. Ten, ten. And eleven
for you.

FONSIA *(She doesn't know)* Just makes you realize.
(Pause.) What'd you do with all the things you had?
You must have had lots of things.

WELLER   I sold them.

FONSIA   It's so hard to part with things you've had so
many years.
       *(Play of the hand proceeds. Again, it is at the director's
       discretion to pace the dialogue to achieve the sense of a
       normally played hand of gin.)*

WELLER   Does the food around here give you diarrhea?

FONSIA   Weller!

WELLER   That's a legitimate question.

FONSIA   Not that I've noticed.

WELLER   You'd notice it.

FONSIA *(Referring to her hand)*   This is a mess.

WELLER   It must be better than this.

FONSIA   What kind of business were you in?

WELLER   I had a marketing and research firm.

FONSIA   I mean what kind of work did you do.

WELLER   Basically, I told people how to run their business. If a company had a product they wanted to

sell—I'd tell them who to sell it to—where to sell
it—and how much to charge for it.

FONSIA   That's something I could never figure out.

WELLER   What's that?

FONSIA   How much to charge for something.

WELLER   What were you selling?

FONSIA   Oh, nothing. But I'd see something I liked . . .
like a lamp . . . and I'd look at the price tag . . . and
it would cost ten dollars. And then I'd see another
lamp just like it and it'd cost over a hundred. There
was just no way of telling.

WELLER   Well, that'll happen sometimes. I remember
when I was just getting started in business, I wanted
a job from this particular company. I was sitting there
in a room with a group of their executives, and finally
the president said, "What's it going to cost us?" Well,
I was afraid to ask for much money at that time. I
thought the job was worth about five hundred—but I
cut it back to four. I was so nervous, I just said the
word, "Four." The president, he turned to one of the
other men and said, "Does four thousand sound in
line to you, Harry?" The guy said, "Yeah, that
sounds about right to me."

FONSIA   (Disbelieving)   Weller, you're making that up.

WELLER   As God is my judge, he said, "That sounds
about right to me."

FONSIA   Did you tell him you meant four hundred?

WELLER *(Disbelief)* What!

FONSIA If it was only worth five hundred . . .

WELLER It was worth whatever he was willing to pay.

FONSIA Finally! Gin.

WELLER Goddamn it. I knew you were keeping jacks. Now what'd I do that for? *(He notes score.)* I gave it right to you. Talking too damned much.

FONSIA You know, I never heard my father say a curse word in his life.

WELLER Obviously you didn't play gin with him.

FONSIA I should hope not. Papa would've never played cards. Didn't smoke, drink, or run around either.

WELLER *(Shuffling the cards)* Admirable. Minor virtues, but admirable nonetheless. You know, I've been thinking more and more lately about my father. Now there was a man who never settled for checker playing in the park. After he retired he still went to the office every morning 'til the day he died at eighty-three. He owned his own company so he could do that. Thank God he had better luck with his business partners than I did.

FONSIA Did you have bad luck . . .

WELLER *(He deals)* One, one. Two, two. Three, three. Four, four. Five, five. Six, six. Seven, seven. Eight, eight. Nine, nine. Ten, ten. Eleven. *(We hear the sound of singing off stage. It seems to be coming from the room directly behind the sunporch.)* What the hell are they doing in there now?

FONSIA Oh, that's probably the songfest.

WELLER I just can't understand this "entertainment."

FONSIA That's a group of singers from the Grace Avenue Methodist Church Choir—some of them sang professionally.

WELLER I don't mean who is singing. I'm talking about this constant need to entertain us. Sometimes I get the idea that they feel like—if they don't have a choir up there, or if they don't have a goddamn magician up there doing tricks or something—then we're all going to drop dead right in front of their eyes. En masse. Then they're going to feel guilty as hell, because deep down, they know that the Grace Avenue Methodist Church Choir could've kept us alive at least another night.

FONSIA I thought the magician was pretty good.

WELLER He poured milk all over the floor.

FONSIA He made it disappear. I know it was a trick, but he poured it in the newspaper and it did disappear.

WELLER It went all over the floor. I was in the first row, I saw it.

FONSIA Well . . . you couldn't see it from three or four rows back.

WELLER That's why magicians like to play old age homes. Half the audience is shaking so goddamn bad they can't focus, and the other half's asleep. *(Long pause as their attention returns to the game.)* Now what're you looking for? . . .

FONSIA   Well, I'll tell you . . .

WELLER   *Don't* tell me!

FONSIA   I wasn't going to tell you.

WELLER   *(He fingers two cards in his hand)*   It's one of these two cards . . . I know that much . . . and I have a feeling the one I discard is going to be the one you want. *(Pause.)* Well . . . here goes nothing.
   (WELLER discards. FONSIA looks at the discarded card and smiles, then picks it up.)

FONSIA   You were right, Weller . . . gin.
   (WELLER bangs his cane to the floor, then, hands on hips, he delivers his line in controlled but genuine exasperation.)

WELLER   Good God, Fonsia!

BLACKOUT or CURTAIN

SCENE 2

(The time is one week later—again Sunday afternoon, visitors'
day. The setting is the same as Scene 1. It is a beautiful sunlit
day, with shafts of sunlight piercing the dusty quiet of the sun-
porch. As the curtain comes up, we see WELLER *standing stage*
right, leafing through a magazine. He appears bored as he
drops the magazine to the table, and, seeing nothing else of
interest, walks to the bookcase stage left—behind the porch
swing. His limp seems somewhat more pronounced than before.
Again, his cane is constantly in hand or under arm. Upon
reaching the bookshelf he scans the titles. Finding something of
interest on the bottom shelf, he stoops to leaf through the book.
This partially obscures him from view behind the porch swing.
The french doors rear center stage open, and again we hear the
sounds of visitors greeting relatives in the room directly off
stage. FONSIA *enters through the french doors. She walks to*
center stage, notices the cards on the card table, and looks
around the room, puzzled at not seeing WELLER. *Now we see*
WELLER *peer out over the porch swing.* FONSIA *is unaware of*
his presence.)

FONSIA   Weller? . . .

WELLER *(Singsong child's voice)*   Ally, Ally, in free . . .

FONSIA *(She shrieks)*   What!

WELLER *(Continues singsong)*   You didn't find me.

FONSIA   Weller, have you gone crazy?

WELLER *(He gets to his feet with the aid of his cane)*   Well, I must admit that's a very appealing thought at times . . . but unfortunately, this time I've done nothing more bizarre than select a book . . . *(He gestures.)* from the bottom shelf.

FONSIA   For a minute I thought you'd lost your mind.

WELLER   No. Although this place inspires a certain looniness.

FONSIA *(It occurs to her)*   This is practically the first time I've seen you to talk to all week.
   (FONSIA sits down in the glider.)

WELLER   Since I met my Waterloo at gin.

FONSIA *(She laughs)*   That was fun.

WELLER   Perhaps you'll grant me a rematch this afternoon.
   (WELLER walks to glider.)

FONSIA   I'd love to.
   (The noisy commotion of the visitors should be quite audible at times throughout this porch swing conversation.)

WELLER   Listen to them in there. *(Pause.)* Every visitors' day it's bedlam around here.
   (WELLER sits in the glider.)

FONSIA   Thank God they don't come out here.

WELLER   Oh, a couple of them stumble out here every now and then. *(Pause.)* A few weeks ago, Gladys Mayes' daughter and son-in-law brought her out here on the porch.

FONSIA   Isn't that a tribe.

WELLER   They didn't have the children with them—but they talk so loudly. Like the old lady's deaf. Hell, there's nothing wrong with her hearing. When she's out here alone, she tells me not to make so much noise shuffling the cards.

FONSIA   She's thin as a rail.

WELLER   They had brought a sandwich out here to her . . . tried to get her to eat it.

FONSIA   She won't eat a bite. I don't know what keeps her alive.

WELLER   They had a coloring book too. Wanted her to occupy herself coloring.

FONSIA   Poor soul—she just sits to the window all day. Coloring would be something for her to do.

WELLER   Well, she'd have no part of it. Then they started talking about me . . . as though I wasn't even there! Like I was a piece of furniture or something. At one point her daughter said, "See, that nice man amuses himself playing cards." I couldn't believe it! I looked at her . . . and in that loud voice she said, "Don't we, sir."

FONSIA   What did you say?

WELLER   I didn't answer. I was dumbfounded. Here this woman is defining my life . . . in one sentence! Or at least she thinks she is . . . and I'm supposed to sit there and agree with her. (To himself in irony.) That nice man amuses himself playing cards.

FONSIA   I don't think she meant it that way, Weller. She probably just wanted Gladys to see that there are things to do other than stare out the window.

WELLER   Why use me as the model retiree, for Christ's sake?

FONSIA   Weller, she wasn't talking about your life. My Lord, look at all the things you've done . . .

WELLER   No . . . but she was talking about my life the way it is now. I'm still alive, damn it!

FONSIA   Well, I hope to tell you.

WELLER   Still, I don't know. Maybe I *am* a little jumpy. I just don't know how to act with people anymore. I'm unsure of myself . . . rusty. There's nobody around here to have a decent conversation with anyway. You're the only one I talk to.

FONSIA   I know. It's awful. You'd think there'd be somebody you'd like to talk to in a place that has as many people as they have here.

WELLER   Half of them are catatonic, for Christ's sake. And sometimes the ones who do talk make you appreciate the ones who don't.

FONSIA   The complaining?

WELLER   Yes.

FONSIA   Have you ever heard so many aches and pains in your life? *(She mimicks.)* My Lord, child, my back is killing me.

WELLER   I know her. Or, I can't see as far as from here to that door. What can you do? It's either that or listen to the help talk to you like a child.

FONSIA   Isn't it the truth. Do you know I never take "my" medicine. No, I take "our" medicine. Time to take "our" medicine, Mrs. Dorsey.

WELLER   I say the hell with it. To hell with all of them.

FONSIA   That's what I say, too.

WELLER   Fonsia Dorsey! Your father would roll over in his grave.

FONSIA   I didn't say it . . . You said it, Weller.
(Both laugh. WELLER with some difficulty gets out of the swing. He stands and looks at his watch.)

WELLER   *(Mock seriousness)*   Do you know what, Mrs. Dorsey? It's nearly three o'clock and we haven't amused ourselves yet.

FONSIA   *(Mock seriousness)*   Oh, my goodness . . . I think I'm feeling faint.

WELLER   I'll amuse you immediately. *(He takes her hand and helps her from the swing. They walk toward the card table.)* At our age that can only mean one thing . . . I'll get the cards.

FONSIA   *(Playfully scolding)*   Oh, Weller.

WELLER   A couple of hands of gin, Mrs. Dorsey—and you'll feel as good as new. *(FONSIA starts to sit in the same chair as Scene 1. WELLER assists her to the other chair.)* Why don't you try that chair this time.

FONSIA   Oh, all right . . . Now, I hope I remember how this goes.

WELLER   From the way you played last time, I don't think you're going to have any trouble whatsoever. (WELLER *makes out the score sheet.*) Let's see, Weller, Fonsia . . . Weller, Fonsia . . . Weller, Fonsia.

FONSIA   You know, my family's never called me anything but Fonsie.

WELLER *(He shuffles the cards)*   Fonsie?

FONSIA   Yes.

WELLER   Why in the world would they change Fonsia to Fonsie?

FONSIA   Beats me.

WELLER *(Spelling)*   F-O-N-S-I-A . . . right?

FONSIA   Yes . . . you spelled it right.

WELLER   Fonsia, Fonsie. That's an unusual name.

FONSIA   I know, I don't have any idea where they got it.

WELLER   Which do you prefer?

FONSIA   Oh, it don't make any difference to me.

WELLER   All right . . . I'll call you whichever comes to mind first, how's that?

FONSIA   That'll be fine.

WELLER *(Dealing ritual)*   One, one. Two, two. Three, three . . .

FONSIA   "Fons" means "source" in Latin, I believe.

WELLER *(Louder)* Four, four. Five, five. Six, six. Seven, seven. Eight, eight. Nine, nine. Ten, ten. And eleven for you.

FONSIA   Why do I get eleven and you only get ten? I know you told me that last week, but I swear I've forgotten.

WELLER   That's because I dealt and you'll make the first play . . . which will be a discard. Get your cards organized—*(Pause.)* All right, now go ahead and discard. *(She discards.)* O.K., now the game is underway. You have ten cards and I have ten cards.
      (Card play; two discards.)

FONSIA   I swear this game relaxes me.

WELLER   Gin's a very relaxing game. I used to play for hours on end on business trips. I had it all figured out—San Francisco to Chicago . . . two Hollywoods. Los Angeles to New York . . . four Hollywoods. New York to Los Angeles . . . five Hollywoods. Headwinds. You always get headwinds flying west.

FONSIA   Well now, all that time you played gin then didn't seem like you were frittering your life away. Why should it be any different now?

WELLER   Well now. That's a good question. *(He pauses, then matter-of-factly and looking directly into* FONSIA's *eyes.)* I don't know.

FONSIA *(Purposely studying her cards)* We don't want to talk about that now anyway.
      (Pause.)

WELLER Have you played?

FONSIA No. I'm trying to figure this out.

WELLER Well, come on, play a card.

FONSIA Oh, all right . . . I'll knock with three.

WELLER *(Sharply)* You told me you'd never played this game before.

FONSIA You explained the part about knocking last week.

WELLER Yes, and if I remember correctly, you were rather hazy about it.

FONSIA No, I understood it. I just said I was going to stick to the gin part of the game at first.

WELLER Well, I don't think we have to worry about your memory anymore.

FONSIA That was right, wasn't it?

WELLER *(He is counting his holding)* Exceedingly. Twenty . . . thirty, forty, forty-three, forty-six . . . forty-eight! *(*WELLER *marks the score pad, forty-eight, then remembers* FONSIA's *three points.)* Minus your three . . . *(He notes score pad.)* . . . gives you forty-five.
    *(*WELLER *gathers the cards and begins to shuffle.)*

FONSIA *(Leaning back in her chair)* Lord, this chair's killing my back. *(Laughs.)* I sound like Mrs. Leala in there now.

WELLER It doesn't seem to be hurting your gin game any.

FONSIA I'm going to have to remember to bring a pillow out here to put behind my back. *(FONSIA takes interest in the way WELLER shuffles the cards.)* My soul. Would you look at that. I can't get over how you shuffle those cards.

WELLER *(He deals)* It's not that difficult.

FONSIA Lord save us—If I tried that, the cards would be flying every which way.

WELLER *(Dealing ritual)* One, one. Two, two. Three, three. Four, four. Five, five. Six, six. Seven, seven. Eight, eight. Nine, nine. Ten, ten. Eleven. *(At the completion of the deal, they both pick up their cards and study their hands.)* What a mess.

FONSIA Do you like stewed tomatoes?

WELLER No.

FONSIA I have never talked to anyone who did.

WELLER They serve them often enough here.

FONSIA I can't understand that. With all the wonderful vegetables there are in this world.

WELLER Dieticians aren't noted for their imaginations.

FONSIA Honestly, I think I could do better than that Mrs. Gib . . . Gib*ran*, Jibran . . . what's her name?

WELLER *Gib*ran.

FONSIA Gibran. Gin!

WELLER *(Piqued)* For God's sake, Fonsia, I just dealt the cards!

FONSIA   I know. I got everything I needed right away.

WELLER *(He notes score pad)*   That seems to happen a lot with you. Let's see, I've got twenty . . . forty-two, plus you get twenty-five for the game . . . gives you sixty-seven. That puts you out in the first game and gives you a sixty-seven leg on the second. Goddamn!
   (WELLER *gathers the cards and begins to shuffle.* FONSIA *peers at the score sheet.*)

FONSIA   You didn't get any points at all in that game, did you?

WELLER   No. No, Fons*ia*, I didn't get any points at all in that game.

FONSIA   That's too bad.

WELLER   It's been two weeks now—that I haven't won a game.

FONSIA   Well, I'm sure you'll win one soon.

WELLER *(He deals the cards)*   I'd say the percentages are definitely starting to favor me. *(Dealing ritual.)* One, one. Two, two. Three, three. Four, four. Five, five. Six, six. Seven, seven. Eight, eight. Nine, nine. Ten, ten. Eleven.
   (FONSIA *puts her hand to her head. She looks disturbed for a moment.*)

FONSIA   Goodness. I just had the dizziest feeling in my head.

WELLER *(Concerned)*   Are you all right?

FONSIA   Yes, it's gone now. I think it's those pills they're giving me. I don't think they hit me right.

WELLER Do you know what they're giving you?

FONSIA I'm not real sure. Seems like it's a different prescription, though.

WELLER You'd better check with your doctor—I mean your own doctor—not one of these welfare quacks.

FONSIA *(Mild panic)* I'm not here on welfare.

WELLER *(Clarifying)* I didn't say you were . . . I just said you'd better get somebody to check that medicine . . . that's all.

FONSIA I didn't mean to jump at you . . .
      (Pause.)

WELLER Play your card. When you got dizzy just now . . . did things get kind of unreal . . . distorted?

FONSIA No. Just a dizziness, like I was going to fall off the chair there for a minute.

WELLER Sometimes I'll be sitting in my room . . . or even out here . . . and everything will take on a dreamlike quality. People, the room, everything . . . like it's not really happening. At first I could snap out of it . . . almost immediately. But then, a couple of times, it hit me and I couldn't shake it. This feeling of sheer terror came over me. God, I didn't know what to do. So I'd sit there panic-stricken. For no reason at all! People around me would go about their business, I don't think they even knew I was having a problem. And then it would pass.

FONSIA That isn't a thing in this world but nerves.

WELLER Whose discard? *(He thought it was FONSIA's and*

was calling her to action. Suddenly he realizes it is his discard and he does so quickly to cover his embarrassment.) Is it mine?

FONSIA   I believe so.

WELLER   I'll tell you, it's one of the worst feelings I ever had in my life.

FONSIA   I went through something like that years ago with my divorce.

WELLER   How did you get over it?

FONSIA   Time.
            (WELLER looks directly at FONSIA.)

WELLER   Just time?

FONSIA   Just time.
            (Pause.)

WELLER   Play a card. *(Pause. Terse.)* Well . . . are you going to play one?

FONSIA   *(Unaffected)*   All right.
            (Pause.)

WELLER   I should knock while I've got a chance. You're probably sitting over there with gin already.

FONSIA   Not quite.
            (Pause.)

WELLER   Nothing. Nothing. Nothing.
            (Pause.)

FONSIA   There it is. Gin!

WELLER   *(Peeved resignation)*   Goddamn it! I just don't

know what to say. I'm stuck with one. You're the luckiest person I've ever seen play gin in my life.
(He notes score then gathers the cards and shuffles.)

FONSIA You *should've* knocked.

WELLER Hindsight is twenty-twenty.

FONSIA You would've really gotten me. I was waiting for a queen. I didn't think I'd ever get it.
(WELLER shuffles the cards.)

WELLER What???

FONSIA I said I thought I'd never get that queen.

WELLER *(Irritated)* Do you mean to tell me you held queens throughout that entire hand?

FONSIA That's what I'm saying. I had those two queens, so if you had knocked, you would have beaten me. Do you see?

WELLER *(Angry)* Fonsia—that is dumb! That is just dumb gin. *(To himself.)* Holding a face card that long. I just can't believe it. *(Dealing ritual.)* One, one. Two, two. Three, three. Four, four. Five, five. Six, six. Seven, seven. Eight, eight. Nine, nine. Ten, ten. Eleven.

FONSIA *(She discards)* I won the game, didn't I?

WELLER Oh, for God's sake. Don't try to relate how you play gin to the fact that you've won a few games.

FONSIA What do you relate it to?

WELLER *(Voice raised)* To one of the most incredible runs of luck I've ever seen in my life!

FONSIA Lord, Weller. I can't help it—don't shout at me for mercy's sake.

WELLER I'm sorry I raised my voice. It's frustration . . . nothing more. Frustration.
(Pause—They play quietly for ten or fifteen seconds.)

FONSIA Have you had any of your things turn up missing since you've been here?

WELLER You mean stolen? Damn right I have—three-hundred-dollar watch!

FONSIA My Lord! I hadn't heard about that. Did you call the police?

WELLER Sure I called the police. They came out here, took my name and address . . . told me it happens all the time.

FONSIA That's awful. You'd think they could do more than that.

WELLER Well, it would be pretty naive to think they were actually going to come out here and solve the case. What are they going to do . . . run around fingerprinting people?

FONSIA I guess you're right. They've stolen just about everything they can get their hands on . . . but you can't prove a thing.

WELLER 'Course not. If they paid anything, they might get some decent help around here. But no . . . they're too cheap for that.

FONSIA They got Mrs. Burgoyne's new gown the other night. That's the third gown she's had stolen.

WELLER I know.

FONSIA Now, Weller, don't get mad at me . . . all I've
done is sit here and play the cards the same as you.

WELLER Have you got gin again?

FONSIA Yes.

WELLER *(Loses control)* Jesus Christ! Do you have to win
all the goddamn time??? I mean it. Can't you lose just
once???

FONSIA Honestly—I'm not trying to do this.

WELLER You're not even trying. How reassuring.
(WELLER *gathers the cards and starts to shuffle, then, realiz-
ing he forgot to note score, he begins to do so.)* Oh hell,
now I've forgotten how many I was stuck with. Oh
. . . It was a bundle, I'll just make it fifty. Whatever
it was, puts you out in the second game . . . let's
see, seventy-six and twenty-five . . . wait a minute,
goddamn, couldn'ta been fifty. Musta been forty.
Gives you . . . ninety-one. Christ, I've never seen anything like it. You're incredible.
        (WELLER *resumes shuffling the cards.)*

FONSIA Weller, I don't want to go through this every
time I win. I'd sooner not play.

WELLER *(Indicating score pad)* But look at that. Go to
hell.

FONSIA I can't help it.

WELLER Oh, I get it. You can't help it if I don't know
how to play gin . . . is that it??? Well, let me tell
you . . .

FONSIA   Weller, I'm going to quit if you keep it up.
*(*FONSIA *moves to leave.* WELLER *grabs her.)*

WELLER   Awh no! You're not going to quit on me now.

FONSIA   Would you want to play cards if someone were shouting at you all the time?

WELLER   All right. I'll try to watch my temper. *(Dealing ritual.)* One, one. Two, two. Three, three. Four, four. Five, five. Six, six. Seven, seven. Eight, eight. Nine, nine. Ten, ten. Eleven. But I'll tell you something, Fonsia . . . it's not just me. This is enough to drive anyone up the wall.
(She organizes her cards, they begin the play of the game.)

WELLER   Finally. A decent hand.

FONSIA   I've got a good one, too.
(Discard.)

WELLER   *(Red-faced with emotion)* You've always got a good one.
(Discard.)

FONSIA   You take it too seriously—Lord, it's only a game. *(Two discards.)* Weller, you're getting so red in the face I'm afraid something's going to happen to you.

WELLER   I get that way sometimes. Look, you've got diabetes—I've got something else—play a card. *(She discards and he refers to her discard.)* That won't help.

FONSIA   I don't want you to have a *stroke* right here in front of me.

WELLER I'll worry about the stroke—you just worry about your cards. *(FONSIA discards. WELLER observes it carefully.)* No help. *(WELLER places his hand on the stack of cards.)* Any five, any six, or the seven of clubs. *(He looks at card.)* Shit.
> *(He discards and FONSIA picks up his discard.)*

FONSIA *(Discards then discovers she has gin and blurts out)* I've got gin.

WELLER *(Disbelief)* I don't believe it! Let me see that. *(He watches FONSIA as she displays her cards on the table. Complete rage follows.)* AW BULLSHIT! BULL-SHIT! *(He gets to his feet and stomps away from the table—then stomps back to look once again at the cards.)* AWH JESUS CHRIST. LOOK AT THAT SHIT!!!
> *(With the word "Shit" he takes his hand and sweeps the cards wildly into the air. FONSIA recoils, not knowing what will come next. WELLER then throws the entire table over.)*

FONSIA *(Fear)* Weller.

WELLER JESUS CHRIST ALMIGHTY!!!

CURTAIN

ACT TWO

SCENE 1

(It is the following evening shortly after dinner. The setting is the same. The room is lit by table and standing shade lamps appropriate to the decor of the room. In the background we hear the clatter of dishes and conversation, as apparently a few late diners are finishing their meals. As the scene opens the french doors rear center stage open and WELLER *appears in the doorway.)*

WELLER   She's probably out here. *(*WELLER *closes the door securely, then turns and looks about the sunporch.)* Fonsia. Fonsie. She might be out in the garden. *(*WELLER *walks to stage right front and peers into the audience, squinting his eyes to see in the darkness.)* Fonsie. Fonsie, is that you out there? *(Pause.)* Answer me.
   *(*FONSIA *is in the far right aisle, several rows back into the audience.)*

FONSIA   What is it, Weller?

WELLER   I wanted to talk to you. It's getting pretty dark out there—you'd better come in.

FONSIA   I'll be in, in a little while. *(Pause.)* Why don't you just go on.

WELLER   I'll just sit out here until you're ready to come in.

FONSIA   Weller, I just wanted to be alone for a

while—out here . . . not in my room.
(FONSIA starts making her way to the stage.)

WELLER   I didn't mean to disturb you, Fons*ie*— honestly, I don't mind sitting here waiting.

FONSIA   No. You're right, it is dark out there now. It was so pretty before—with all the spring flowers.

WELLER   I'll get right to the point, Fonsia . . . I owe you an apology.

FONSIA   Yes, you do.

WELLER   *(As though quoting or reading)* All right . . . I am embarrassed by my own behavior yesterday and I sincerely apologize.

FONSIA   I can't tell whether you're joking or whether you really mean it.

WELLER   Of course I mean it. What do you want me to say, that I behaved like a complete ass?—I'm sorry that I upset you . . . and I'm sor . . . I'm sorry, that's all.

FONSIA   It frightened me. I don't think you realize how much your temper affects people.
(FONSIA sits on the glider.)

WELLER   I'm sure it can be rather awesome at times— but there's nothing to be afraid of.

FONSIA   I don't think I'm so much afraid of you for what you're going to do to me. I just don't know what's going to happen next. When you threw that table . . .

WELLER Oh, that was nothing. It wasn't directed at you anyway.

FONSIA It still frightened me.
(WELLER *sits next to* FONSIA *on the glider.*)

WELLER Now, Fons*ie*, let's be realistic about this. Look—except for the couple of times that I lost my temper, I think we've thoroughly enjoyed each other's company.

FONSIA I enjoy your company, Weller . . . but you can't play gin.

WELLER *(Suddenly angered)* What??? What the hell do you mean I can't play gin. Lord, woman, I was playing gin . . .

FONSIA No, no. No, Weller. I didn't mean you can't *play* gin. I just meant you can't play without losing your temper.

WELLER Jesus. Next thing you know you'll be thinking you're some sort of expert, for Christ's sake.

FONSIA My lands, no. Lord knows, I'm no expert. *(Moderate pause, then playfully.)* I just play like an expert. *(Laughs.)*

WELLER *(Stung)* Oh, God. Now she's done it. *(WELLER is quickly on his feet, limping briskly to the bookcase.)* Goddamn it, where are those cards.

FONSIA *(Hurriedly)* I was teasing, Weller. Weller. As the Lord is my savior . . . I was only teasing you.

(WELLER *has taken the cards from the bookshelf and is rummaging around in the bookcase for his score pad.*)

WELLER   Lots of people tease like that. They say exactly what the hell they mean—then they say, "I was only kidding." Where's my score pad, you can't keep anything around this place!

FONSIA   Now, Weller, I'm not going to play any gin with you.

WELLER   Oh come on, Fons*ie*, for God's sake.

FONSIA   I mean it.

WELLER   All right, don't play. Go on back in there with all those glassy-eyed old bastards.
(*He sits down.*)

FONSIA   You shouldn't talk that way about them—you're part of this thing here, too, you know.

WELLER   Yeah. Well, if that's the case . . . I'm the part of it that's breathing. Don't you kid yourself, this isn't anything more than a warehouse for the intellectually and emotionally dead. Nothing more than a place to store them until their bodies quit.

FONSIA   God, you're cynical.

WELLER   It's not cynical. It's a fact, that's all.
(*WELLER shuffles the cards and starts playing solitaire. He snaps the cards down emphatically as he plays each one.*)

FONSIA   Well, I'm sure glad I don't look at life that way. It's just the mercy of God that we're able to get around a little better than they are. They're just sick, that's all.

WELLER   They're not half as sick as the ones who put them here. And they're not a third as sick as this bunch that's supposed to be taking care of them.

FONSIA   Which side of this thing are you on, anyway. Sometimes I think you're just looking for a fight.

WELLER   I'm just looking to mind my own business.

FONSIA   And you've got a horrible temper . . . and a sarcastic streak . . .

WELLER   *(Defensively)*   So what. *(Cuts her off.)* If I were you I wouldn't be talking about anybody else's shortcomings.

FONSIA   What's that supposed to mean?

WELLER   Well, neither one of us is winning any popularity contest out here on visitors' day.

FONSIA   Oh. I see. No one visits me so I'm an evil person.

WELLER   Ya ever hear of Ty Cobb?

FONSIA   He played baseball.

WELLER   That's right, Ty Cobb played baseball. He played baseball for twenty-four years. You know how many of his teammates showed up for his funeral? *(Rhetorical pause.)* Three! Kinda makes you think that Ty Cobb may have been something less than a warm, loving human being, doesn't it?

FONSIA   Maybe.

WELLER   Well sir, he's three ahead of us on visitors.

FONSIA   What are you driving at, Weller?

WELLER   Why doesn't your son visit you?

FONSIA   I told you. He lives in Denver. I thought you understood that.

WELLER   Then why aren't you in an old age home in Denver. Or you'd think at least he'd come here to see that you're comfortable and that it's a decent . . .

FONSIA   I don't want to talk about this anymore. The Sunshine Ladies are going to be here tonight. I think I'll go in and talk to them for a while.
          (FONSIA *walks to the french doors, then pauses.*)

WELLER   Help yourself.
          (*He loudly snaps a card on the table.*)

FONSIA   I suppose you think they're so many jerks too.

WELLER   Now I never said anything like that. *(Pause.)* They're a hellava lot more sincere than some that come out here. Like that group who came out looking for substitute grandparents. What'd they call that?

FONSIA *(Uncertain)*   Ex . . . extension family???

WELLER   Yes, that's it. Extension family—no . . . it wasn't extension . . .

FONSIA   Extended!

WELLER   EXTENDED! That's it! Unitarians. Wanted to—psychoanalyze everything, for Christ's sake.

FONSIA Weller, I wish you wouldn't take the Lord's name so much.

WELLER What's it going to be . . . gin, or the Sunshine Ladies?

FONSIA *(Starting to turn)* Oh, I think I should go in.

WELLER Hell, they're not going to be here for an hour or more.

FONSIA Well . . . I still think I'd better . . .

WELLER All right, goddamn it, go ahead. I don't see how you can stand it in there. The same damn empty look, face after face. You ought to see them on the days when the bed linens are changed . . . maybe you have. All lined up in those wheelchairs, all up and down the halls . . . like rows of wrinkled pumpkin heads . . .

FONSIA Maybe we could play a few hands . . . you're just going to pester me 'til I play anyway.

WELLER Well. What the hell else is there to do?

FONSIA Not much, I guess.
    (FONSIA *starts to sit down.)*

WELLER Oh, would you get the score pad? Thank you.

FONSIA I'm so tired of the TV. And all Mrs. Leala wants to talk about is her funeral arrangements.

WELLER You won't find a hotter topic of conversation—I don't care who you talk to. Not around here.

FONSIA My mother was that way. As far as I can remember, funerals were the only social life she had.

(WELLER *notes names on score pad.*) If this isn't the pot
calling the kettle black. Here I sit talking about the
same thing they are.

WELLER *(Lightly)*   That's what happens when you get
away from playing gin too long. Atrophy. Next thing
you know, you'll be staring out the window all day
long.
   (Laughs.)

FONSIA   Weller, you're imposs . . .

WELLER *(Dealing)*   One, one. Two, two. Three, three.
Four, four. Five, five. Six, six. Seven, seven. Eight,
eight. Nine, nine. Ten, ten. And eleven for you.
   (FONSIA picks up her cards.)

FONSIA   Now if I win, don't you shout at me.

WELLER   Fons*ie*, I fully expect you to win . . . and I
promise I will do my level best not to rant and rave
about it.

FONSIA   All right now, I'm going to hold you to that.

WELLER   I swear, Fonsie, you get yourself upset about
the silliest things.

FONSIA *(I have reason)*   Well . . .

WELLER   Well, you do.

FONSIA   Sometimes, I guess. *(Pause as they play the
cards.)* You know something used to worry me sick
when I was working . . .

WELLER   What's that?

FONSIA Now, this really is silly. But I was always afraid I was going to misspell a word.

WELLER *(Laugh)* Now there's a novel fear for you.

FONSIA It's the truth. I *had* to go to work after I divorced Walter. *(Pride.)* I worked as an apartment manager. 'Course, I didn't have any education to speak of . . .

WELLER You've got a good mind.

FONSIA Still, I was always afraid they'd find out.

WELLER Find out what?

FONSIA I put down that I had graduated high school.

WELLER Oh Lord—Who cares whether you graduated high school or not. For God's sake. How old are you anyway?

FONSIA Seventy-one.

WELLER Seventy-one! And you're afraid that somebody's going to find out that fifty years ago you didn't graduate with your class. My God, Fons*ie*.

FONSIA Weller.

WELLER *(It occurs to him)* You've got gin.

FONSIA Yes.

WELLER I know. I know it. *(He gathers the cards.)* I'm stuck with eight. *(Impatient.)* You know when you get gin you're supposed to put the discard face down.

FONSIA I'm sorry.

WELLER   It's not a big deal. It's just the way the game is played, that's all. *(He notes the score.)* Let's see, that's eight plus twenty-five, gives you thirty-three. And, of course, I get my customary goose egg.

FONSIA   Weller, I can't help it. I'm sorry.

WELLER *(Shuffling the cards)*   Don't be sorry for me, for Christ's sake.

FONSIA   I just wish you could win one.

WELLER   You play your best, damn it! I won't have you trying to lose . . . just to appease poor Weller. I'm one of the best . . . One, one. Two, two. Three, three. Four, four. Five, five. Six, six. Seven, seven. Eight, eight. Nine, nine. Ten, ten. Eleven . . . damn gin players you'll ever see and I sure as hell don't need any help from you.

FONSIA *(A warning)*   All right, Weller. *(FONSIA organizes her hand and they begin the play of the hand. They play two discards, then FONSIA continues resolutely. Note: WELLER picks up both discards.)* Transferred!!!

WELLER   What?

FONSIA *(Determined)*   Transferred!

WELLER   What the hell are you talking about?

FONSIA   How many r's are in the word "transferred?"

WELLER *(Matter-of-factly)*   "Transferred". . . two.

FONSIA   Hah!

WELLER *(Uncertain now)*   Three. What the hell . . .

FONSIA *(Triumphant)* Three!

WELLER Three.

FONSIA Three! There are three r's in the word "trans-ferred." You know that I had to look that word up every time I spelled it for twenty-five years. 'Course, you get a lot of people transferred in the apartment business . . .

WELLER You're not paying any mind to what you're doing.

FONSIA I am too.

WELLER You just gave me the jack of *(whatever he picks up from discard stack)*.

FONSIA I couldn't use it.

WELLER *(Anger building)* I know . . . but I just picked up a jack no more than thirty seconds ago. You knew I was keeping jacks . . . why'd you just give me another one?

FONSIA *(Angry too)* Because! I'm not keeping jacks.
(WELLER *slaps his cards to the table and gets out of the chair.)*

WELLER Well, I got the gin . . . so you'll be pleased to know that your little plan worked.

FONSIA *(Exasperated)* What plan??? In the name of the Lord.
(WELLER *is now up and pacing—building a rage.)*

WELLER I told you not to lose on purpose, by God, and I meant it! I don't need you to let me win.

FONSIA   I'm not letting you win. *(She gets out of the chair.)* I wish you could see yourself right now, Weller.

WELLER   Where are you going?

FONSIA   If you could see yourself you wouldn't act this way.

WELLER   *(Loudly)* I SAID, WHERE DO YOU THINK YOU'RE GOING!

FONSIA   It's late, Weller . . . I think we should just go on in.

WELLER   *(Forcefully)* Now Fonsia, you sit right, back down over there. *(WELLER takes her arm and directs her back to the chair. He does this forcefully but not violently.)* We're nowhere near quitting! In fact we're just getting started.

FONSIA   Besides, you said you wouldn't get this way.

WELLER   *(He helps her into the seat—still angered)* I'm not *getting* any *way*. All I'm asking you to do is play the cards the way you normally would . . . and try to win!
     (WELLER gathers the cards.)

FONSIA   Weller, I don't like this. Really . . . I think you should see one of the doctors when they come by.

WELLER   Hand me those cards over there.
     (She hands him cards. WELLER shuffles.)

FONSIA   Maybe the doctor could give you some pills.

WELLER   Don't you worry about the doctors. You just play the cards—and play them right. *(WELLER shuffles the cards.)* I'm going to get to the bottom of this, Fonsia. No . . . *We're* going to get to the bottom of this, because you're going to help me. What we're going to do is . . . we're going to find out exactly what force is at work here! There's a reason why you constantly draw the precise card you need—and you do, come hell or high water—and I'm going to find out what that force is. *(Dealing.)* One, one. Two, two. Three, three. Four, four. Five, five. Six, six. Seven, seven. Eight, eight. Nine, nine. Ten, ten. Eleven.
     (WELLER gets his cards arranged, ready for play. FONSIA has not picked hers up yet.)

FONSIA   Weller, I'm not feeling well.

WELLER   Play your cards, damn it! *(Pause—WELLER continues in affected tone.)* I'm sorry. Please play your cards.

FONSIA *(She picks up the cards)*   This is ridiculous.

WELLER   I don't care if it's ridiculous or not! Discard. *(She discards at his command.)* All right. Now I'll discard . . . and you'll pick it up. Won't you??? *(She picks up his discard.)* She did!!! I told you she would. Didn't I say she would?

FONSIA   Weller, who are you talking to?

WELLER   To myself. To me and my little man. You see, there's a little man sitting right there. *(He motions.)* Now I'll discard—and—it's going to be the exact card Fonsia wants. *(He discards and she reluctantly picks it up.)* What did I tell you! Christ, she controls my mind.

FONSIA *(She shakes her head from side to side)*   Oh Lord.

WELLER   This time I'll trick her. I'm going to discard this caaaard . . . and, no. At the last minute I'm changing my mind—to discard this card. And she doesn't take it. By God, I think I've found the answer. You've been reading my mind, haven't you, Fons*ia*? What are you? Are you some sort of witch? No, that's not it. *(He leans toward her.)* I know what it is. It's divine intervention. That's what it is . . . DI-VINE INTERVENTION!

FONSIA   Stop it, Weller.

WELLER   Well, it is, isn't it? *(Discards.)*

FONSIA   It's late. I think we should go in.
    (FONSIA *puts her cards face down on the table.)*

WELLER   You've got it, don't you? You've got gin.

FONSIA *(Weary)*   No, Weller, I don't have it.

WELLER   You've got to say so when you get it now. Because I'll be damned if I want you sitting there with gin in your hand waiting for me to go out.

FONSIA   Believe me, I'll tell you. I just need one card—when I get the one card I'll tell you.

WELLER   Well sir, you won't be getting any more help from me.

FONSIA *(Very weary)*   Well, I got it. There it is—gin. Now can we quit?

WELLER   Who gave you that card??? *(He hits the table.)* I want to know who gave you that card. *(WELLER hits the table again. FONSIA just stares at him.)* GOD GAVE IT TO YOU, DIDN'T HE??? *(FONSIA says nothing.)* DIDN'T GOD GIVE YOU THAT CARD???

FONSIA   Yes, Weller. God gave me the card.

WELLER   *(Spitting venom)*   Don't you patronize me—you bitch!
    (FONSIA instinctively slaps WELLER across the face. There is a stunned silence.)

FONSIA   *(Fiercely)*   Just who do you think you're talking to—man. *(The word "man" is delivered with contempt.)*

WELLER   All right, I shouldn't have called you that.
    (FONSIA starts to get up and leave.)

FONSIA   I'll not sit here and have you call me names like that.

WELLER   *(Undiminished authority)*   No. No. Don't go. I said I was sorry—*(Rising anger.)* Now that should be enough!

FONSIA   I've had enough of this whole thing.

WELLER   *(Demanding)*   I said don't go!
    (FONSIA steps to the french doors.)

FONSIA   I'm going to call one of the nurses.
    (WELLER feverishly gathers the cards.)

WELLER   No! No! Wait a minute! Wait! What would you want to do that for? What are you going to tell the nurse, "I'm being held hostage by a maniac who's forcing me to play gin."

FONSIA I should tell her something.
(FONSIA *stands at the french doors.*)

WELLER *(Composing himself)* One more hand! Just one more hand! I promise.

FONSIA *(Distressed)* This is so upsetting.

WELLER If I can just get these damned cards straightened out. (WELLER *looks at the score sheet and starts to note the score.*) What the hell's the score? Fonsia, a thousand—ten thousand, screw it. (*He sweeps the score sheet aside and picks up his cards.*) Look. We'll play this one more hand. Just this one, then we'll quit. *(Pause.)* Come on, Fons*ie*, I promise this will be the last hand. *(Dealing ritual.)* One, one. Two, two. Three, three. Four, four. Five, five. Six, six. Seven, seven. Eight, eight. Nine, nine. Ten, ten. Eleven.
(*With great weariness* FONSIA *picks up her hand of cards, examines them and discards.*)

FONSIA I hope this is quick.

WELLER Do you mean I didn't deal you a perfect hand? I must be slipping.

FONSIA Just play your cards, Weller.

WELLER *(Mimicking)* Just play your cards, Weller. Well, aren't we getting tough.

FONSIA Not tough. Just tired. Very tired.

WELLER Well, all you have to do . . . (*He slams his drawn card on the discard pile.*) Goddamn it! (*Pause.*) All you have to do is win this one real quickly . . . and we can go in. (*He repeats the slamming action as above.*

FONSIA *picks up his discard.*) Son-of-a-bitch! (FONSIA's *eyes flash at this.*) I'm talking about the cards.

FONSIA   No, you're not.
>   (FONSIA *plays in silence.* WELLER *seems to be hanging on each card he draws. As he picks up each card, he curses it in disgust and slams it to the table.* FONSIA *ignores his rage. Each comment following is made in reference to each card as it is drawn. The pauses indicate* FONSIA's *draw.*)

WELLER   Aw for Christ's sake, come on. *(Pause.)* Goddamn it!

FONSIA   Every other breath you draw has to be a curse word, doesn't it?

WELLER   *(Pause)* Shit! (FONSIA *draws her card, puts it in her hand, then, saying nothing and without discarding, she displays her hand face up on the table. She doesn't look up.* WELLER *leans across the table to scrutinize the cards, then shouts.*) SAY IT!!! (FONSIA *says nothing.* WELLER *gets up and walks a few feet from the table, then turns to her and in a shouting, accusatory tone, continues.*) YOU'VE GOT IT. GODDAMN IT—SAY IT!!! *(Still there is no response from* FONSIA. *He limps angrily back to* FONSIA— *leans over her and shouts directly into her face.*) SAY IT!!!

FONSIA   *(Barely audible)* Gin.

WELLER   CHRIST, YOU CAN SAY IT LOUDER THAN THAT. I CAN HARDLY EVEN HEAR YOU.
>   (FONSIA *suddenly assumes* WELLER's *level of rage, shouting spittingly in his face.*)

FONSIA *(Shouting)*   GIN—GODDAMN IT!!! GIN!!!
> (WELLER *wheels toward rear center stage and stomps with a heavy limp toward the french doors. He turns toward* FONSIA *to deliver the following line.*)

WELLER   All right. We'll go in.
> (WELLER *exits through the french doors.* FONSIA *is left alone on the stage. She sits absolutely motionless as though shellshocked. She is both angry and frightened. Hold this briefly.*)

BLACKOUT or CURTAIN

SCENE 2

(The setting is the same. The time is the following Sunday afternoon. The sunporch is once again bright—but only to provide contrast for a darkening of the room brought about by an afternoon thunderstorm. The storm descends shortly after the scene begins. Claps of thunder rumble occasionally. As the scene opens, WELLER *is seated, reading a magazine. At the sound of voices from the living room he gets to his feet and briskly walks to the french doors. He opens the door and peers in, then closes it with resignation. He walks slowly back to center stage and slumps back into the chair—no longer interested in the magazine. He seems listless. The french doors quietly open and* FONSIA *enters. She sees* WELLER, *stops for a moment, then, ignoring* WELLER, *she walks to the porch swing with deliberation.* WELLER *starts at catching the glimpse of* FONSIA *out of the corner of his eye, but says nothing.* FONSIA *sits down in the swing, still ignoring* WELLER. *She swings with her eyes fixed at a point straight ahead.)*

FONSIA *(Matter-of-factly)* Mrs. Mayes just told me my sister Hattie was waiting for me on the porch—came to see me.
(Pause.)

WELLER *(Offering)* I thought you said she lived in Ottawa.

FONSIA I did.
(Pause. WELLER *feigns renewed interest in the magazine.)*

WELLER   Well sir, no one's been out here.

FONSIA   I didn't expect there would be.
  (Pause.)

WELLER   How've you been?

FONSIA   Mrs. Mayes isn't all that clever, you know.

WELLER   You can't pay any attention to what she says.
  She doesn't even know what's going on half the time.
  *(FONSIA stops swinging and looks accusingly at
  WELLER.)*

FONSIA   Oh, she got the message straight all right . . .
  *(WELLER realizes that FONSIA is staring at him and
  finally acknowledges this.)*

WELLER *(Defensively)*   What am I supposed to say?

FONSIA   She said, "Mr. Martin *told me* to tell you your
  sister Hattie's waiting on the sunporch."
  *(WELLER slams the magazine down and directs his total
  attention to FONSIA. He is on his feet.)*

WELLER *(Barks)*   Oh . . . I didn't tell her any such
  thing.

FONSIA *(Snapping)*   Who the Harry do you think you're
  kidding, Weller??? Do you suppose I would have be-
  lieved that? A sister I haven't seen in fifteen years—I
  would have come out here looking for her . . . all that
  just to . . .

WELLER   Well, you didn't believe it—so what the hell
  are you complaining about.

FONSIA It's disgusting that you would go that far just to get me out here.

WELLER I don't give a damn if you never come out here.

FONSIA Oh yes you do. I know why you want me out here. It's that blasted card game—you just can't get that off your mind.

WELLER I haven't asked you to play all week, have I?

FONSIA I haven't talked to you all week.

WELLER So what! I could've asked you to play—if I were so all-fired hot about it.

FONSIA It's been on your mind . . . I can tell that.

WELLER What's so strange about that? Does that make me some sort of nut?

FONSIA You just can't drop it. It was a game, Weller. You lost—it's over—so forget it.

WELLER Well . . . suppose I do want to play you again.

FONSIA Nothing doing! The minute you lost, it'd be the same thing all over again. I may be old, but I'm not crazy.

WELLER (*Angered*) I'm not *crazy* either!

FONSIA I've never seen a man get so . . . so wild . . . over a game of cards in my life. It's not natural, Weller, there's something wrong.

WELLER I know all about how you think something's

wrong with me. They called me down the office last Tuesday and said they were thinking about having a psychiatrist come out here and talk to me. Do you know what they could do if he says there's something wrong with my mind? They could have me committed to the state mental hospital. The very fact that you complained makes me a troublemaker.

FONSIA   You could need help and not know it—there is such a thing as that, you know. All I was trying to do was to help you.

WELLER   Goddamn it, I don't need your help—and don't you go judging me.

FONSIA   All right . . . suit yourself. I just felt as long as you've got some money it couldn't hurt to have you talk to someone who might be able . . .

WELLER   Got some money??? Who told you I had money?

FONSIA   Well, you did. I mean . . . you had your own business . . . and you did well, I thought. *(Pause.)* Flying around the country, I just assumed . . .

WELLER   Oh hell, I *did* do well. You're right. *(Pause.)* I built that goddamn business. And if I'd a had a little better luck in picking partners, I'd probably still have it. I'm not sure Henderson had all that much to do with it. But Clark! Christ, he literally had me thrown out of my own business!

FONSIA   How could he do that? Didn't you get anything?

WELLER   It's too complicated—Yes, I had some money.

I *HAD* OVER FORTY-SEVEN THOUSAND
DOLLARS! But I made the mistake of getting
sick—then I made the mistake of getting well. I
stayed at Belair Convalescent two-and-a-half years
after my heart attack—The money just ran out. Then
I had a relapse—had to go to the hospital for four
days—and those bastards at Belair wouldn't hold my
bed! I didn't have any money left, so Belair didn't
have to take me back. I was "placed" here. PLACED!
By some lowly, brainless bastard at the welfare department. And now you're trying to have me declared
some sort of . . . of personality *(Thunder.)* problem,
around here.

FONSIA Maybe I shouldn't have said anything . . .
NO, if I didn't say anything, the next thing you
know they'd find one of us out here on the floor.

WELLER Oh, Fonsia, don't be ridiculous.

FONSIA You may think it's ridiculous—but I'm the one
who's been getting shouted at and pushed around.
And the way you look at me when you get like that
. . . I'm just not sure what you might do.

WELLER What do you think I'm going to do? Hit you
over the head?

FONSIA I just don't know.

WELLER You just don't know??? Good God, you make
harsh judgments, Fonsia. I'm a potential murderer?
I'm crazy. I'm vulgar. According to you I'm a hope-
less sinner for taking the *Lord's* name all the time. I'm
dishonest in business . . .

FONSIA   I didn't say that.

WELLER   What?

FONSIA   That you were dishonest in business.

WELLER   The hell you didn't. Remember the guy who paid me four thousand . . .

FONSIA   No, you said yourself it was only worth five hundred . . .

WELLER   I said it was worth whatever he was willing to pay.

FONSIA   Well, you're the one has to live with it.

WELLER   You know what's wrong with most people in the world? . . . they've got a mother who's just like you.

FONSIA   That's the most insulting remark I've ever heard in my life.

WELLER   God. I'll bet your son has had a hard time . . .

FONSIA   Weller, that's personal and it's none of your business. Now . . .

WELLER   I know why Larry doesn't visit you. I know why it is now . . .

FONSIA   WELLER . . .

WELLER   It doesn't have a damn thing to do with Denver . . . or distance . . . or job . . . or anything else like that. I know what it is now. You've made him feel like the lowest piece of crap on earth for so long he can't stand the sight of you. He hates you.

FONSIA THAT'S NOT TRUE! AND I WON'T
HAVE YOU TALK TO ME LIKE THAT!!!

WELLER He's never done anything right, has he? He's
never done a thing on this earth to *please you*, has he?

FONSIA STOP IT, WELLER. I'M WARNING
YOU.

WELLER He doesn't even live in Denver, does he?

FONSIA That's the craziest thing I ever heard . . .

WELLER You are guilty of lying? Fonsia is a liar . . .
because your son lives right here in town and you
know it!!!

FONSIA He does not hate me!!! He doesn't hate me!!!

WELLER Then why doesn't he visit you? Why does he
totally ignore his *own* mother?

FONSIA He . . . He just doesn't bother, I guess, he just
doesn't bother. How did you know he lives here?

WELLER I didn't. I was guessing.

FONSIA Guessing??

WELLER Yes. Guessing.

FONSIA Guessing! YOU BASTARD. YOU
BASTARD.
  (FONSIA *weeps hysterically as she pounds her fist on*
  WELLER's *chest.*)

WELLER Fonsie. Fonsie. Fonsie. I'm sorry. I'm sorry.
(Pause.) Lord, it's cold out here. It's getting darker
too. That storm's getting closer.

FONSIA *(Sitting down)* Weller . . . I did lie to you. *(Pause.)* I'm on welfare too.

WELLER *(Sitting down)* I guess we just lived too long, Fonsia.

FONSIA I had a little money—but with the hospital bills and trying to look after myself . . . plus I still had that little house over on Ash Street I was trying to run . . . 'Course, you can't expect your children to give up their lives. But I fixed his wagon on that house, by God. That went straight to the presbytery!

WELLER Oh. Well, I didn't mean all that I said before . .

FONSIA They can do whatever they want with it. But it's one thing he won't get.
(There is a flash of lightning and a loud clap of thunder rumbles in the distance. We hear the heavy downpour of rain.)

WELLER Here comes the rain.

FONSIA I know who he takes after. His father was as rotten as they come—I always hoped Larry'd be different. I did the best I could. I struggled to raise him by myself—trying to hold on to what little we had. And after all I did for him, what's he up and do— about five years ago, but try and look up his father!!! "Over my dead body!" I told him, "You do that and you've seen the last of me." Sometimes I think he does hate me . . . I don't know.

WELLER Fonsie, you're just getting yourself all upset. There isn't a thing in the world you can do.

FONSIA   I know. I shouldn't get this way.

WELLER   Just relax yourself. You're only doing yourself
harm. What you need is to get your mind off him. *(A
loud clap of thunder rumbles overhead accompanied by a
brilliant flash of lightning. At the sound of the thunder, the
lights flicker, actually going out momentarily.)* Good
God. I hope that didn't hit the home! *(Standing.)* No,
guess it just hit a power line or something. What the
hell is that? Look at that. The goddamn roof's leaking
again. They were supposed to have renovated this
place five years ago, and look at that! The roof leaks.
The walls are so damn thin you can punch your
finger right through them. The heat doesn't work.
This is a goddamn slum . . . that's just what it is . . .
a goddamn slum. It's falling apart! Look at that! *(A
wall fixture near the french doors catches WELLER's eye. It is
a light switch that has been screwed on at a cockeyed angle.)*
There's a perfect example of *exactly* what I'm talking
about. That switch is on there at damned near a 45-
degree angle. *(Comic slur.)* I don't know how drunk a
man would have to be to think that's straight up and
down.

FONSIA   I know it's so.

WELLER   I guess it's going to rain all day.

FONSIA   I think so . . .

WELLER *(Sitting down)*   Well, come on, I'll play you a
hand of gin.

FONSIA   You know, Weller, you can be such an . . . an
enjoyable person to be with—you've got a wonderful

sense of humor . . . If it wasn't for that damn gin game.

WELLER My goodness, Fonsia. Such language.

FONSIA Weller, I've played all the cards I'm going to play.

WELLER Now, Fonsie, I'm not going to argue with you. We're playing gin!
(*FONSIA gets to her feet.*)

FONSIA That's it, Weller! You're not going to drop this gin game business . . . and I'm not going to play. So there's no reason for us to sit here and fight over it. I'll just go on in.

WELLER You stay right where you are.

FONSIA It's the only thing I know to do.

WELLER What do you mean, it's the only thing you know to do?? You came out here, didn't you?
(*WELLER is now on his feet.*)

FONSIA Yes, I did. But certainly not to play gin. All I wanted . . .

WELLER All you wanted to do was manipulate me! We've been playing your game . . . NOW WE'RE GONNA PLAY MINE.

FONSIA I'm not even gonna get into this with you, Weller.

WELLER The hell you're not. You knew your sister Hattie wasn't here. You saw through my little plan to get you out here—but you came out anyway. *(They start back toward gin table.)* You can't tell me you didn't enjoy beating me game after game, watching me get angrier and angrier.

FONSIA   Taking a chance on Lord knows what kind of violence!

WELLER   Don't be ridiculous!

FONSIA   I don't think I'm being ridiculous when I say that. When you lose that temper of yours, I believe you're capable of anything.

WELLER   Oh, for Christ's sake, would you get off of that and come back over here and sit down!

FONSIA   No, Weller. I'm going in.

WELLER   Goddamn it! I'm not going to let you go in there. You'll tell 'em I'm crazy.
   (WELLER grabs FONSIA roughly by the arm.)

FONSIA   Let me go! Get your hands off me!
   (FONSIA tears away from WELLER's grasp.)

WELLER   Quiet! For Christ's sake, they'll hear you!

FONSIA   I hope they do.

WELLER   You *do*, don't you. You'd love to get in there and tell them I've been out here shouting at you again. That'd do the trick. *(Pause.)* VINDICTIVE! That's what you are . . . VINDICTIVE! *(Pause.)* Screwed your own son out of that house—just so you could get even with him . . . for God knows what reason.

FONSIA   *(Inflamed)*   That's my business, damn it! You

can just shut up about it! Who do you think you are anyway??? Maybe I had good reason for what I did. You don't know the situation. The only thing you care about in the world is that damn gin game. You're the one who's so vindictive . . . saying anything to me, just because I won't play . . .

WELLER   SIT DOWN! SIT DOWN!!!
(WELLER *menacingly indicates the chair.*)

FONSIA *(Fierce anger)*   Goddamn you! All right, goddamn you!!!
(FONSIA *sits down.*)

WELLER   We'll play one hand . . . and you play to win, goddamn it!
(WELLER *sits down.*)

FONSIA   Don't you worry about that, mister.

WELLER   All right, by God . . . you've got it! This is it! This is the game!
(WELLER *quickly shuffles.*)

FONSIA   Deal.

WELLER *(Dealing)*   One . . . (WELLER *starts to deal* FONSIA *the first card in the customary fashion, then changes and deals himself the first card.*) One, one. Two, two. Three, three. Four, four. Five, five. Six, six . . .

WELLER and FONSIA   . . . Seven, seven. Eight, eight. Nine, nine. Ten, ten. Eleven.

WELLER   I'm going to beat you this hand . . . By God, I'm going to beat you.

FONSIA *(Acidly)* I don't know what makes you think it's going to be any different this time.

WELLER Don't you get smart with me.

FONSIA I'm not getting smart—it's the truth. If you played this game so well, you would have beaten me long ago.

WELLER *(Incensed)* SHUT UP, GODDAMN IT!!! I'll show you who's going to win, by God—you just concentrate on your cards!

FONSIA It's *your* discard!

WELLER I KNOW IT'S MY DISCARD!

FONSIA *(Acidly)* I hope you *do* lose. I hope you lose so badly . . . God.
   (The sound of a choir singing in the living room becomes noticeable but not distracting.) ·

WELLER Jesus Christ, another choir. That's all we need is another choir. *(Pause.)* Why don't you pick up my discard and gin on me. You can't do it, can you? It's going to take a lot more than luck this time.

FONSIA You've got to be the victim of bad luck, don't you, Weller?

WELLER Watch your cards.

FONSIA Because if it wasn't bad luck, it'd have to be something else, wouldn't it?

WELLER I said watch your cards!

FONSIA It'd have to be something like—maybe you

think you play gin a whole lot better than you really play it . . .

WELLER   Goddamn it, you're asking for it, Fonsia!

FONSIA   If it hadn't of been *bad* luck with your business partners then it probably would've had to been something like *bad* judgment . . . or worse yet, maybe they were simply better businessmen than you were. It could've been . . .

WELLER   YOU SHUT YOUR FUCKING MOUTH! You don't know the first thing about . . .

FONSIA   DON'T USE THAT WORD IN MY PRESENCE!

WELLER   I'll use any FUCKING word I please.

FONSIA   You're just like that one I got. A filthy foulmouth. That was his word. There I was with a two-year-old baby hearing such filth.

WELLER   I'm sure he had a damn good reason for using it.

FONSIA   I fixed his wagon. He came home one night with half a load on . . . and I had everything he owned right on the street. I mean *right on* the street! That was the end of that!

WELLER   I would've knocked your damn teeth in . . .

FONSIA   Yes. And I would've had you in jail so fast it'd make your head spin.

WELLER   Bullshit!

FONSIA Don't you think I wouldn't. Besides, Walter was too much of a coward to do that anyway.

WELLER You don't have too many kind things to say about the men in your life, do you?

FONSIA I'll admit, when it comes to men, I've been very unlucky.

WELLER You've been what???

FONSIA I said, haven't had much success . . .

WELLER You've been UNLUCKY.

FONSIA All right . . .

WELLER Sounds like you've had that same kind of bad luck you've been telling *me* about. It had to be bad luck, because if it wasn't bad luck, it would've had to been the fact that maybe it was *you*. That maybe you're a rigid, self-righteous, vicious . . .

FONSIA All right! You made your point! Just be quiet and play your cards.

WELLER All right, by God. *(Pause.)* Play. *(Pause.)* Well, are you going to discard?
(She discards. WELLER *draws from stack and contemplates the card at length, anguishing over which card to discard.)*

FONSIA You have some nerve complaining about the time I take.

WELLER You want this one. *(Holds out a card regretfully.)* This is the one you want. And I'm going to

have to give it to you, too, damn it.
(WELLER *discards disgustedly.*)

FONSIA *(Contempt)*   That was stupid. You just gave me
the other queen three plays ago. I'll take it.

WELLER   I didn't have any choice, idiot!

FONSIA *(Livid)*   Don't you ever call me an idiot, you
. . . Don't you ever call me an idiot, you . . .
FUCK!!! (WELLER *looks at* FONSIA *incredulously.*) I've
never used that word in my life.

WELLER   Play a card.

FONSIA *(Slams card down)*   All . . . right! God*damn* you.
(WELLER *picks up her discard.*)

WELLER   Now, by God, we'll see who was stupid. One
card. One card. (WELLER *discards, then* FONSIA *draws a
card.*) Now we'll see who's an *idiot!*

FONSIA *(Seething)*   Shut your mouth!
(FONSIA *discards.* WELLER *draws.*)

WELLER   Be it. Be it. Goddamn! So close!
(FONSIA *draws a card, looks at her hand, then goes to
discard.* WELLER *sees the card. It's the one he needs. As*
FONSIA *discards, she flips it over and puts it on the
discard pile face down.*)

FONSIA   Gin!

WELLER *(Stunned)*   Gin.
(FONSIA *leans back in her chair and displays her hand
on the table with enormous satisfaction and hate.*)

FONSIA Gin.

(WELLER *leans to see* FONSIA's *hand revealed on the table. There is a slow realization within him.*)

WELLER (*Quietly*) Gin. (WELLER *rises to his feet. His already savage anger is now inflamed to madness. He slams the cane on the chair* FONSIA *has just vacated as he shouts the word "gin."* FONSIA *recoils in terror. She scrambles to get out of the way.*) GIN!!! (WELLER *then slams his cane down across the table with a frightening crack as he shouts the word again.*) GIN!!!

FONSIA Don't hit me! Weller, for God's sake! Nurse!

(WELLER *brings the cane down violently across the table many more times, each time punctuating the action with the continuing chant, until the strength goes out of him. The rage becomes defeat.*)

WELLER GIN! GIN! GIN! GIN! GIN! GIN! GIN!

(WELLER *stands motionless in stunned silence. He stares at* FONSIA, *then slowly turns and walks to the french doors. At the door he pauses, the shoulders slump, then as a sleepwalker he exits slowly.*)

FONSIA (*Pause*) Weller . . . (FONSIA *seems to want to go after* WELLER, *but stops. She has a long moment alone. Then nearly whimpering.*) Oh no . . .

(*She slumps onto the glider.*)

CURTAIN